*"Poetry that bleeds."*

*A. Stout*

While every precaution has been taken in the preparation of this book, the publisher assumes no responsibility for errors or omissions, or for damages resulting from the use of the information contained herein.

CYBERSCOPE 2

**First edition. January 20, 2018.**



ISBN: 979-8201191672

Written by Perry Mark Stratychuk.

# Also by Perry Mark Stratychuk

New Worlds Radiation Game
Bone 2 Bone
Tour of Time's Edge: S.F. Special
Cyberscope: Experiments in Transrealism
Cyberscope 2
The Shadow of the Shaking Tree
Return to the Shaking Tree: Scriptworks

# Table of Contents

For my parents Catherine and Donald.

# PART 1

## NIGHT FEAST

The sweet voice

is complete darkness

The well-turned ankle

a moon's light rising

A half-million francs

a tiny graveyard

The appearance of being half-clothed

only in mind

The hungry hands form

a velvet mouth

A bientot, merci

## CORRESPONDING HUMAN HEADS

purifying

compound eyes

packaging

plasmid rockets

clinical

nutrient baths

testing

dead embryos

## MISS HACKER AN'IZONA
## (SAD REPRISE)

I went out to the City

with some friends

three weeks ago

It was nice and cool up there

I've never eaten such great

junk food

I mentioned I like to dance

but out here the men

(if I can call them that)

are afraid

to dance

with girls

I still don't dance

with punks

or ugly old men

I still wear

Nehru coats

and psychedelic pants

## 1-900-PHOENIX

Reenacting horrors

colliding face to face

evcr-groovy legacy

meters are our fate

do what's cleft undone

pretty time less music

hiding harrowing traits embodied

in fear and presuppositions

## MESSAGE FROM ANDROMEDA

The heart I give

is one untied

one free to hold

free to fly

The heart I give

once apart in two

no longer tears

for want of you

The heart I give

need not return

a gift of permanence

my soul you've earned

The heart I give

is yours in time

a love worth wanting

beyond our lives

## HE DID NOT RESIST

drenched hot

by

macabrc mcmories

he squealed

whimpered

and shuddered frantic words

unknown things

witnessed

in the field

great sweeps

of light

where the highway meets the lake

## TWO MOON SKY

Up on the dome

our wine is shared

The night spills down

as free as hair

We reach afar

on moments aware

And return to level

with natural eyes

To split the whole

alone once more

## INTRUDER

Seeds fall

from thc rafters

Thc tree behind

the birds

Pick up

cach absent mind

Rains fall

and I move slowly

Step by step

and up

On the row

and like the rafters

I creak and crack

like wood

Standing still

to see thc birds

ln the nests

they see me

And leave

on my account

To hover

by the window

They hold positions

longed by di Vinci

To hover

and face my guilt

I leave

on their account

Overdrawn

and now due

## REALITY KILL

In upstairs rooms

where sounds of

blue mondays

cringe alone

factories exist

to part painlessly

the best

from the bruises

Lost promises

and distorted images

are held in-gag

minutes from letdowns

nervous touching

of hero and hip

leave stairwells corrupt

with the rain of moonlight

## PERIMETERS OF LOVE

The shining cloth

of forgotten seas

lay before me

until we meet

The darkened hood

of starlit sleep

lay over me

and you are far

The soundless noise

of worried dreams

fill my mouth

and you are silent

The sunlight's rise

from a blue sheet spreads

in soft comfort

and you are nearer

## EXCERPT FROM AN EXPERT HUNTER'S HANDBOOK

What she's

got

you

couldn't spell

Facets of ability

detailed rules

target acquisition

professional reputation

and

two dice...

## SEDUCED IN INK

Gone are worlds

of Suzy Wong

nights of seams

old Hong Kong

Fantasies though

never real

so much less

than what can feel

Between us borth

long over time

posted love

through optic line

Gin and lime

in Buddha's eye

down and out

spill the lies

Your face on screen

in velvet mood

felt in contact

fluid food

## RED SKY SETTING

The sun set red no blue filled sky

The moon felt clean

I walked as sandy darkness fell

I remembered twice the times we met

We sat eating imaginary lunch

We met again and we sought freedom

And this wrould be the last crime

Between us the sun set green

A paramecium sky caked pink with clouds

Reflectant on skin honey neat and sticky

Lightly on the neck afraid of too much

We fell back she asked could I hurt you

I said no and looked for marks

Tangled we ate real food

## CAPTIONS FROM AN ANCESTRAL PHOTO ALBUM

Subject wears:

Mud dresses

pointy-toed shoes

fishnet stockings on colored hose

Pale as death

she refers to day

as sunlight avoids her

She smears sunscreen

on the TV

reading fiction bores her

She writes letters, cats

cats

and sleeps

she lets friends talk at her

She "don't go chasing guys, they don't really matter."

From experience

they don't chase

her either

"I don't compromise."

the caption read

"always look for someone better."

## POP THING

I'm unzipping you

a digital icon

of me

Posing with

my brother

in Diego Garcia

It's the only one

I have

I will need it back

Maybe I'll get replications

you can keep those

when I unzip them to you

In them I'm in a black and white

T-shirt without

a bra

White pants

standing barefoot

I'd just taken of my antique Beatle boots

I think I look

very cool

very hip

## THE TRICK AND IT'S A HARD ONE

People told her she should be a comedienne because she's

very funny with an outrageous and dry sense of humour

others told her she should be an actress because she's a

flamboyant person and not boring for sure she likes

to choose her friends but music is what she wants to get

into if she wasn't so broke she'd play in a band a boss

garage band or a hip and cool blues band she needs music

lessons, and the guys she'd recruit would have to look like

the Rolling Stones in '66 ditto clothes and of course she

would be the leader of the band no trendy outside

influences, she's a loner and knows her "kids would be

artists or musicians..." she can't sing but could get a

vocalist she could write songs and direct she can't read

music but she has a lot in her head with a deep voice like

Cher's.

# THE ARTISTIC ABDOMINAL SURGERY GANG

cold times empty

black leather

toxic wars end in

plastic pirouettes

aesthetic embraces slide off

oiled holovisions

mirrored tears drip on

laser scalpels

hot-rodded books hold up

tubeway queues

cappuccino CDs while

chocolate lubricates

severed fallacies fill

time-woven space

cocoonning grace enlightens

neon etiquette

eyes

# PART 2

## TWILIGHT JESTERS

The last sound of grave

dancers

dig

the colour of shadows

as battles

rage

inward

The justice mirror

motions

a machine

into deep grooves

of a lost Siamese

dreamers land

The spawning growth of

judges

warp minds

to fear forms

as each thorny edge

of national fate

stumbles

## OBLIVIOUS RECEPTORS

Sparking in corners

of fuzzy logic

Almost abandoned

with weeds of silver

Positions and parts

lead in ambient trance

Junior farcasters

watching and touching

The world's ending

in a wired beginning

## COLD CREEP WORLD

Liquid metal rats

scurry

every prison block

on a cold creep world

Gang honors

transport

machine-drawn souls

a luckless filthy tribute

Star gunners

reload

skull-shot blasters

trained on far frozen enemies

Lost teachers of climax

clench

union steel in teeth

2028 years ago from now

## MOMENTARY GLIMPSES OF SILICON AND STEEL

Hyper-media bankers

multi-caress invisible cash

Bitrakers jam-crypto

digit-fed engines

Meta conferences grow

for fingerless fetishists

Fabrics of history

become kid combat systems

Painterly tools

scribe doomed sculptured flesh

Cold characters nibble

in a diner of sad regret

Hot virtual organs

in a bio-soup du jour

## THE GLASS-LIDDED CHEST

Sack after sack

of plaster

and habits of caution

always examine

her

bit of bare backbone

the curtains

draw aside as

the outer door creaks

with

sad proud smiles

of rumours and low

unhurried voices

splashed and

splattered

like an abbattoir

of Persian design

liquid red

as blood

suppcr

without bread

camphor and wine

odours from

half-flagons of

liquid

with unsmoked tobacco

alive inside

a bulky wooden chest

with a lid of

glass

## "SNAKE, THIS IS YOUR TIME."

Stone columns

of my dreams

plot night emissions

in unknown space

Desert city sites

of modest rebellions

house the impossible

and passive killers

## A CONSIDERABLE THRUST TO A DEFENSIVE SKIN

Floating in space

massive squat shapes

layered for defense

sin arrangcments

Combat craft

and rocket packs

thrust pod attackers

enraged planetary systems

The last years of wars

and manned command centres

freefell, like lovers as

uncontrollable victims

Came goblin gunships

of fearsome beings

far more sinister

than particle collisions

Lone pursuit ships were

left virtually defenseless

and clean, fresh of flesh

and bloodletting

## UNCERTAINTY THEATRE

A dream of science

now proven false

Predictable chaos

and imminent redemption

A future order is

natural bad news

Uncertainty theatre

ordered tranquility

## RADIO CONCRETE

I was a highway once

a messenger

for aggravated acquisitions

Until a palace

that blosssomed deep

in the hills

Glowed like a

bitter sense

of dying

Only for a while

it reminded me

of helpless youth

Then from my skin I lost

the gold made into a key

for entrance to the palace

So I solemnly spread

foolish scandals of discouragement

as the distant palace glistened

## THE INFORMATION RAILWAY

Mega-companies

lie

for monopolies to slow

down

your ability to communicate

freely

then bill you

for

your

own

displeasure

## MINISTRY OF ROTTING ENTERTAINMENT

Each cold nighttime claims

when you round bends of pain

no remembrance of riding a reason

Each boggy sun covers

lost squirmers inside

each city, each ending of vision

Good-god-spirits

channel farce on farce

intricate significant sub-plots

Computer-age headwaters of

galactic adventurers intrigue

with revenge on wet metal ass

## A VAMPIRE OF NIRVANA
### *(ON A HIGH GARDEN VISTA BEFORE SUNRISE)*

syringes and cup

wet kitchen table

smells of blood

*and heat*

a face is stiff

so badly rigid

experiments again

*under stars*

explicit impulses

invisible reflections

cups of blood so potent

*a drug*

atop a steel penthouse

600 floors up

a sardonic free, tosses

*a shell*

escape-pod launched

set for some darkside

new life to flesh from

*each blood of one*

## THE GAMMA RAY DIHEDRAL

Our war of blues

a prototype

of nothing

sacred to your dreams

Down a stairway

of pain

the commencment

of wicked games beloved

Its blunt recipe

a measure

of each angry rain

dissolves all falling in love

## BENEATH THE CITY

Machine life and electrical verses

Events rule and data curses

When Power fails

Each headache worsens

As darkness calls

A network rails

Time and funds

Whisper firepower

Savagery and desire

Jack up to re-explode

Cross plazas over

Braided technology

Lashing the back

As frontiers slightly bend

## DRINKING 100 TIMES THE AMOUNT

it'

the lost robot

looks back at

life

fast-paced, lube logged

fragmented

feeling-less

poor lost robot

once part of a

Cola family

it'

witnessed members

of a once great micro-state

drown in niche-war

it'

remembers killing

ruthless assassins

who inspired kid slogans and shirts

robot come home

all is forgivable

## HOPING FOR A SUDDEN FIRESTORM

Each shining message over brass band

music

follows a silence department releasing grimy

samples

as clamking society bulldozes composers

keys

## ENCOUNTERS PENDING

It's thin hands

as true geodesics

implied the ship's

long voyage

To a pre-space Earth

of intelligent icons

awaiting the coming

past hectic hours

A once delicate touch

of sun-starved skin

an alert brightness

of crystallized mechanism

Eschewing suspicion

of human encounter

the visitor awoke

as translation engine

It's flash-frozen remains

now blackened by smoke

an unknown threat

on bare frosted ground

# PART 3

51

## LONG NIGHT ON HARD ROCK

"Recommendation for complete carnage."

I saw that phrase scribbled diagonally across the moss-colored computer tablet. The words untavelled like a lost string of code at the workstation the night I examined the body.

Circling his rag-doll torso flopped forward in the wooden chair I began my task. He faced down with eyes wide, drying as hot air forced itself through the room from the ceramic heater nearby.

It was too hot in here tbr my liking.

I felt sweaty and anxious as I examined the hand still curled round the handle of the small Colt AutoFaze he kept handy.

He hadn't pulled the trigger.

After checking the safety, I tugged the weapon from his clutch and popped out the magazine.

No shells.

It wasn't like a Supervisor to be ill-prepared. Maybe it was the condition he'd been in for the last couple of days. You know that anxious state. The one state that can tip you from dreamy suicide to lucid murder.

I knew it well and I couldn't take my eyes off the results.

The Supervisor was just plain dead. I thought back to our scenescreen

meeting the other day.

"You look a little funny," he said when the electronic image beamed his haggard face into my early morning.

"Well, you know I got these... digestion problems," I said.

He didn't say much after that, at least nothing that stands out in my mind or that I can remember at the moment. It just seemed he had this stare in his eyes. The kind you know means a guy's not coming out with it.

Then again I was probably kidding myself. Maybe I was playing too hard at cheap detective in AsterCity.

The place was a hard-boiled pit ofinvaders and ex-royal subjects that I'd stepped into this time. They were sick from too many Voyages, too many wars. Some three thousand settled on this floating mine and resource foundry. For me, it was just another stop, another job. Yet, people actually lived there and even raised families as far as I could tell. I admit I tried escaping these kinds of responsibilities when I could, though sometime things happen and, hell, he's a good kid. His mother is

too, though she doesn't want me around the place since the class wars, but that's another story.

Anyway this case came at the right time. I needed off Earth A.S.A.P.

still the Supervisor was sort of an old friend.

It was that kind of thinking that made a job like this more dangerous than necessary.

I looked back at him and the black pattern on the floor near his feet. It spread on the carpet like gelatinous red clouds on a New Mars morning. Soon it would soak clean through. The floor below was nothing but a thin coat on the hewn surface of depleted mining rock.

Still, I couldn't avoid the signs. His severed spinal cord just below his neck. The look of surprise in someone who was prepared to do battle, but prepared to die as well. His grip not only held the gun, but the false security in the possession of weapons.

I'd seen that before too, somewhere, some installation, some other world. There were so many. Too many.

Moving away from the desk I stained to see through that darkness in his office that night.

I sniffed at the hot air and figured a "beast" had to to be laying motionless, silent, and somewhere nearby. I smelled only that heat smell, but nothing else.

I hadn't passed anyone or anything on the way up. There was only one lift and one operator.

Then I heard it.

I swore silently as deep and difficult breaths escaped from the dark. They filled the room with strong disgust. Their hoarseness took on its' own shape, its' own mass. Nausea grabbed at me from within the shadows. My senses picked up the sound of a running trickle of fluid like a human urinating. I knew it was both alive and dangerous to the extreme and I doubted I could get out of the office in any normal manner.

I needed the hundred percent solution, an immediate kill. I had to rob this thing of existence, a life it itself had stolen.

You wouldn't think disintegration was necessary for the crime of theft. Of course you don't know the thief. It's a robber that hungers for the marrow of souls. A violator that enters and reaches down into you and claws your sweet memories until they become poison. A toxin that would make you consider turning yourself off like a switch.

At the end, your life probably doesn't flash before you in a whirlwind, but instead creeps up and prods you with regret until you smother. Just maybe there's nothing more to death than the biggest

holiday ftom your troubles, or in my case, everyone else's. And one of these troubles feels damn close.

Say good-bye to the machine of life.

I reached into my holster and switched my weapon to biokill, just case I hit an exterior wall. I didn't want to lose the air in here, even if it was rank.

I breathed deeply.

Blasting the blackness around me felt better than it should've.

So much in fact, I did it twice. Three times.

Moments later it was over.

After a sudden gasp I made it to the door which seemed much farther away than I remembered.

There was no resistance.

Outside the office I slipped into the metallic cage elevator and waited for the operator to take me take me back down to main level. She didn't appear and I wanted off this hard rock, bad. I pushed down on the brown handled lever. Relays kicked. The cage shuddered as it dropped. This day had been long, hard and I spent too much time on sentimentality.

I was even building up something you'd call an appetite. Maybe I could finally catch up on some sleep during the next shuttle jump.There would years in travel time to regroup until I came across my next adversary, the next destroyer.

Somewhere a tentacle lashed out.

The cage-lift slammed still at level one!

The door opened as my gun-hand shook and tensed a trigger-finger.

Before me stood a destroyer.

I fired.

Again and again.

"That's all I remember' I swear'"

"You don't remember then, the operator's scream as she faced your gun?"

"No. I've already been asked these questions."

"I know. You don't recall any claxon sounding, any security forces pursuing you?"

"No."

"Do you remember firing your weapon again at the central foundry?"

"No, but there was another destroyer at foundry control'"

"What did this one look like?"

"Tentacles, feasting, gorging on everything in sight. I could smell it too. Like death, like the reaking disrespect for its' environment I know it had."

"Like the others then?"

"Pretty much, Yeah'"

"What did you do? You said you didn't fire the weapon there."

"I snapped its' spine, same as at the office'"

"So you rid AsterCity of all the destroyers. Is that correct?"

"So far as I know. Any more questions?"

"A couple". Tell me again why you felt it necessary to 'cleanse' as

you put it, the citv of its' destroyers? Whats did they do to make this mission of yours so urgent a need for you?"

"They were already killing themselves, I just helped the poor bastards along. They already ruined their habitat. Plundered it, polluted it. They were wallowing in the filth of their own making'

I couldn't let them move on to the next asteroid or planet for that matter, although there would still be those that would try. They're out there somewhere."

"I see. That'll be all for now."

"Will you be questioning me again?"

"Oh yes, after they move you to the new penitentiary"

"Alright."

"Actually, I did have one more question? May I?"

"Go ahead."

"Can you tell me just who or what these 'destroyers' are specifically?"

"Sure. People."

"Humans?"

"Yes. Why do you ask?"

"I just wondered if you knew."

# Also by Perry Mark Stratychuk

New Worlds Radiation Game
Bone 2 Bone
Tour of Time's Edge: S.F. Special
Cyberscope: Experiments in Transrealism
Cyberscope 2
The Shadow of the Shaking Tree
Return to the Shaking Tree: Scriptworks

# About the Author

**Perry Mark Stratychuk** (born in St. Boniface, Manitoba, Canada) is a filmmaker, writer, musician, poet, and actor. Described in a review as a "*natural artist*", he is a director, cinematographer, and producer in several movie genres such as experimental short film, music video, and documentary. Along with writing *bizarro fiction* and poetry, Perry creates strange **"outsider"** artworks, and can be heard forging eclectic electronic / experimental guitar music for soundtracks and albums as a Canadian electronic drone music pioneer active since 1981. Perry currently resides in Chengdu, Sichuan, China with his wife Sayda, and miniature Schnauzer Aboo.